D0498512

A BIRTHDAY BOOK

WRITTEN AND ILLUSTRATED BY

joan walsh anglund

Determined Productions, Inc.

ISBN 0-915696-01-0
Library of Congress catalog card number 75-10848
Printed in the United States of America
Published by Determined Productions, Inc.
Box 2150, San Francisco, Ca. 94126

Especially for:

. . . . . _Janet_ . . . .

. . . .

. . . . . . _Love_ . . . .

Mother & Daddy Bob

JANUARY

JANUARY 1

To understand
is
to begin to love.

. . . .

JANUARY 2

Eyes that gaze far,
may miss
the sweetness
that is near.

. . . .

JANUARY 3

All snowy is the air,
All twirly-white around,
Like tiny ballerinas
Come to dance in the town.

. . . .

JANUARY 4

In his dreams,
  even the tiniest kitten
    can tiger be.

. . . .

JANUARY 5

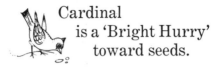

Cardinal
    is a 'Bright Hurry'
       toward seeds.

. . . .

JANUARY 6

People will forgive anything
       but being made
          to appear 'foolish'!

. . . .

JANUARY 7

Snow,
   . . . like Innocence resettled
upon the ancient brow
       of Earth.

. . . .

JANUARY 8

Some men count their profits,
but, *I* count my friends!

. . . .

JANUARY 9

A rag-doll
   is the most comforting
      of friends!

. . . .

JANUARY 10

Though years hurry,
   in my heart
You never change.

. . . .

JANUARY 11

Where it is dark,
    let me bring light.
Where there are tears,
    let me bring laughter.

. . . .

JANUARY 12

How small the box that holds you,
How safely hid, the key,
No one knows the Secret,
   . . . only Memory!

. . . .

JANUARY 13

How good it is to feel
that *someone*
loves
you!

. . . .

JANUARY 14

Today I must finish
what Yesterday began.

. . . .

JANUARY 15

Wisdom calls,
. . . but do *I* listen?

. . . .

JANUARY 16

Each day
is a Surprise-package
. . . waiting to be opened!

. . . .

JANUARY 17

Sleep, my baby, sleep,
. . . in the soft cradle
of your dreams.

· ·

JANUARY 18

There is always
more Work
Than there is Time
in which to *do* it!

· ·

JANUARY 19

Because I could not have it
    I put my hope aside . . .
And, later, when I looked again,
    My little Dream had died.

. . . .

JANUARY 20

The Mind may Wander
. . . a Vagabond,
While *we* must stay,
sedately, at home.

. . . .

JANUARY 21

The white delight
of being "snowed-in",

. . . No School today!

· ·

JANUARY 22

What we Do
states
what we Believe.

· ·

JANUARY 23

We can never catch Time,
 He runs too swiftly!
But Memory has a slower step,
 . . . Let us grasp *his* coat-tails!

. . . .

JANUARY 24

Contentment
 is a soft couch
upon which
 I dream.

. . . .

JANUARY 25

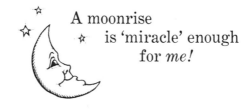

A moonrise
   is 'miracle' enough
    for *me!*

. . . .

JANUARY 26

Child, Child,
   Time for bed
A pillow awaits
   your golden head.

. . . .

JANUARY 27

It is always difficult
    to be Sensible . . .
Therefore,
        I seldom try it!

. . . .

JANUARY 28

All things
    are possible
To those
    who believe!

. . . .

JANUARY 29

January is a silver circus,
    oh! see the white clowns twirl!

. . . .

JANUARY 30

The ruby of a cardinal
    upon a winter bough,
the sudden joy of color
    when all is missing now.

. . . .

JANUARY 31

Each day is an awakening . . .
Let me be truly "awake"
to this Day
that shall never "be" again!

FEBRUARY

FEBRUARY 1

Love is the warm nest
    from which Happiness
        is hatched.

. . . .

FEBRUARY 2

By the warm fire,
  our old cat
     dreams,
  in furry circles.

. . . .

FEBRUARY 3

 Time and I
are enemies,
...We do not agree!

. . . .

FEBRUARY 4

Say you love me. Say you care
... and when I need you,
you'll be there.

. . . .

FEBRUARY 5

Snow dresses
each holly-bush
in diamonds!

. . . .

FEBRUARY 6

Read,
and a new World
opens!

. . . .

FEBRUARY 7

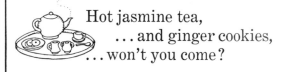

Hot jasmine tea,
    . . . and ginger cookies,
. . . won't you come?

· ·

FEBRUARY 8

Love cannot be tamed,
    trained, or kept on a leash.
. . . it is obedient to no one.

· ·

FEBRUARY 9

On a rainy day,
      it's best to stay in bed!

. . . .

FEBRUARY 10

Will I ever
      know the Answer?
When will all the pieces fit?

. . . .

FEBRUARY 11

If you need me,
...call!
I will always answer!

. . . .

FEBRUARY 12

No happier companion
than a dream!

. . . .

FEBRUARY 13

How numb
    a joy becomes
at the frost-touch
        of Indifference.

· ·

FEBRUARY 14

To one who is gentle as the dove,
    I give my heart,
    ... my trust,
        ... my love!

· ·

FEBRUARY 15

No one works harder
for you
than yourself.

. . . .

FEBRUARY 16

I've decided
to give up
Worry!

. . . .

FEBRUARY 17

The River, who is busy,
  looks up,
    and envies
The Mountain...who is still.

. . . .

FEBRUARY 18

The road to joy
 leads always to *you!*

. . . .

FEBRUARY 19

Sleeping
is what I do
best!

. . . .

FEBRUARY 20

Destiny's hand
is stronger
than all our careful plans!

. . . .

FEBRUARY 21

I have no new words,
        ...only the familiar trio,
                ..."I love you!"

. . . .

FEBRUARY 22

We reach out
        toward Love,
as the tendrils
        reach for Sunlight,
        ...that we each may *Live!*

. . . .

FEBRUARY 23

A letter
     Is the thought
          of a friend,
. . . sealed,
     and sent to you!

. . . .

FEBRUARY 24

It is true. I have not been wise.
But, it is also true . . .
          I have not been
               "unkind"!

. . . .

FEBRUARY 25

Never more 'Alone'
    than in a crowd!

· ·

FEBRUARY 26

Take my hand.
    We have so many things
        to find...together!

· ·

FEBRUARY 27

Who sees a rose
without a happier
heart?

. . . .

FEBRUARY 28

All things
work well
with Love.

. . . .

FEBRUARY 29

When it is stormiest without,
stay most still within.

. . . .

MARCH

MARCH 1

When Spring hums
   at my window,
   ... I cannot worry!

. . . .

MARCH 2

Little Flower
   what secrets could you tell?

. . . .

MARCH 3

Butter from the Jersey cow,
Honey from the bee,
Corn-bread from the oven . . .
Won't you come for tea?

. . . .

MARCH 4

A joyful heart
can weather any storm .

. . . .

MARCH 5

I have come too far
to give up *now!*

. . . .

MARCH 6

It is never
too late
to Love!

. . . .

MARCH 7

Hello baby chick,
    just out of the shell,
so fuzzy and yellow,
    I wish you well!

. . . .

MARCH 8

Today went all so quickly,
    . . . did I "notice" it?

. . . .

MARCH 9

Oh, my friend,
    ...I shall miss
        the joy you brought!

. . . .

MARCH 10

How many conversations
    have begun
because of dogs
    ...and children?

. . . .

MARCH 11

Jonquils,
  . . . a sunny sea
in which I wade!

. . . .

MARCH 12

Happy is the man
  who enjoys his work.

. . . .

MARCH 13

Say hello
  to a new day
...in which
    Anything is possible!

. . . .

MARCH 14

I've always tried
  to be helpful.

. . . .

MARCH 15

Buttercups
 are the bright coins
  of the meadow.

. . . .

MARCH 16

I am
 an
  amateur
   optimist!

. . . .

MARCH 17

Steady as a heartbeat,
   the thought of you remains.

. . . .

MARCH 18

How quietly a Love can live.
   It takes so little room,
To keep its candle in your heart
   As Light against the gloom.

. . . .

MARCH 19

 Hello dear Spring,
   You kissed me,
      and I am "warm" again!

. . . .

MARCH 20

Never a morning . . . Never a Day,
   that I don't miss you
      in some little way!

. . . .

MARCH 21

Sunset spreads her
　　cloak of rainbow,
And invites us each
　　to Wonder.

. . . .

MARCH 22

You
are important
to me!

. . . .

MARCH 23

Oh Bunny!
    Why did you leave?
...one white-cotton hop
        and you were *gone!*

. . . .

MARCH 24

Wake up, Winter,
        hurry away!
Spring is waiting,
        for us, to play!

. . . .

MARCH 25

Distance cannot separate
hearts
that still
remember!

. . . .

MARCH 26

When I have lost my way,
a crocus winks,
and I "believe" again.

. . . .

MARCH 27

A kitten
   is a sudden "meow"
...when milk is poured.

. . . .

MARCH 28

We stand poised
   on the last hour of Winter,
A March moment
   before Frost melts into Spring.

. . . .

MARCH 29

A sweet smile
        invites
            sweet words.

. . . .

MARCH 30

Bunny, always hopping . . .
        always in a hurry,
Bunny, never stopping . . .
        Doesn't your mother worry?

. . . .

MARCH 31

I bring a bright bouquet
of wishes,
that I have chosen
just for you.

· ·

APRIL

APRIL 1

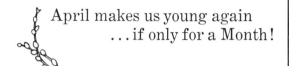

April makes us young again
...if only for a Month!

. . . .

APRIL 2

Kindness
is so simple a deed,
...yet,
how we avoid it.

. . . .

APRIL 3

Hope is a rocket
    that men
        may ride to the stars!

. . . .

APRIL 4

The rain is over...
    but she has left
silver memories behind
    in every springtime
        furrow and field.

. . . .

APRIL 5

Bluebell,
...... did you ring?

. . . .

APRIL 6

Why is Spring? How did it come?
It didn't fly. It didn't run.

Where is Spring? How can you tell?
It whispers, first, down in the dell!

. . . .

APRIL 7

Who
does not
need
love?

. . . .

APRIL 8

I hurry to the thought of you,
as to a warm nest,
where I shall find haven.

. . . .

APRIL 9

Easter Eggs of brightest hue,
Yellow, pink, and green and blue,
Hidden here, for me and you,
Hurry!... Let us find a few!

. . . .

APRIL 10

A glad song
quickens
any task.

. . . .

APRIL 11

Spring has begun
        her yellow circus,
and we are *all* invited!

. . . .

APRIL 12

A good friend
    is a lasting delight!

. . . .

APRIL 13

Rain
signs her
silver autograph
upon my
windowpane.

. . . .

APRIL 14

How warm is the kiss of Spring,
. . . it awakens every sleepy bulb
and blossom.

. . . .

APRIL 15

Be honest with yourself,
and no man can find you false.

. . . .

APRIL 16

Glory in the morning!
    Glory in the sunset!
. . . and in between,
        the Dazzling Miracle
            of Now!

. . . .

APRIL 17

Though small,
        below,
the Hyacinth
    repeats
      the sky's
        blue prayer.

• •

APRIL 18

Even the Storm
    could not frighten
       . . . were *you* "near."

• •

APRIL 19

Each thought
   is Mind's momentary Home.

. . . .

APRIL 20

I'll be Sensible
      . . . tomorrow!

. . . .

APRIL 21

The wind whispers . . .
the brook speaks . . .
Let *us* listen !

. . . .

APRIL 22

Amidst the loud
and clambering crowds,
in the stillness of my heart,
. . . I find *you!*

. . . .

APRIL 23

How azure would be Infinity
   with *you* along to share!

. . . .

APRIL 24

Heaven is
near
in April.

. . . .

APRIL 25

So sad,
    . . . can't play!
Too bad,
    . . . Rainy Day!

. . . .

APRIL 26

Your eyes
        speak *more*
            than you know.

. . . .

APRIL 27

I'm happiest
When I'm
    complaining!

. . . .

APRIL 28

Spring is a Mother
    gently awakening her
        children again and
            prodding them
                to growth.

. . . .

APRIL 29

Oh! April!
...You break my heart
with your tear-drops!

. . . .

APRIL 30

Yellow, orange,
        red, and green,
purple, blue
        ...in Rainbow seen!

. . . .

MAY

MAY 1

The twelve months
are Sisters,
. . . but the fairest
is May!

. . . .

MAY 2

Each apple tree in full bloom,
is like a great pink bouquet
offered to the Sun.

. . . .

MAY 3

So dark is the Day
    when *you're* away . . .

So bright is the minute
    when you're back 'in' it.

. . . .

MAY 4

Along my walk,
    rows of sedate tulips,
like nuns,
    nodding in meditation.

. . . .

MAY 5

 Lily of the valley
     hiding in the shade,
shyly bringing Beauty,
     gentle May-Time Maid.

. . . .

MAY 6

Open the door!
   . . . a Morning
      is waiting!

. . . .

MAY 7

Never wait
  to do a kind thing.

. . . .

MAY 8

Up in the tree
  there's a wee little nook,
Just right for me,
  and my bear,
  and my book!

. . . .

MAY 9

And now, at my doorstep,
pansies
    lift their purple eyes
      again!

. . . .

MAY 10

When the heart is full,
  how inadequate
    seem the 'words'
      that tumble forth!

. . . .

MAY 11

I am always astonished
at how much
I do not know.

. . . .

MAY 12

How-do-you-do, Miss Primrose!
Welcome back, Bluebell!

. . . .

MAY 13

These yellow stars!—
these crowds of sunny faces!
. . . these Daffodils!

. . . .

MAY 14

Who plants a garden
begins Delight
for others.

. . . .

MAY 15

To be free,
    we have only
        to 'let go'!

. . . .

MAY 16

I, myself,
    am my own best friend,
    . . . and worst enemy!

. . . .

MAY 17

Life is easier
    if you take it
        one minute at a time.

. . . .

MAY 18

How casually
    we find the precious things
      of our lives,
     . . . work,
       . . . friends,
         . . . and lovers.

. . . .

MAY 19

Oh! hear the Spring thunder!
. . . in small wars
behind the hill.

. . . .

MAY 20

On a dewy pink morning
we forget our black midnights!

. . . .

MAY 21

"Life is in the little things"
... that is what the Robin sings.

. . . .

MAY 22

Small expectations
    by Joy will be blest,
But Heartache accompanies
    the ambitious quest.

. . . .

MAY 23

Fate
  has made us what we *are*
We
  must make ourselves
    what we "wish" to be!

. . . .

MAY 24

Each seed
  is a new life.
Oh, packet!
  . . . sprinkle!

. . . .

MAY 25

Flowers, like children,
   remind us again
      that life continues!

. . . .

MAY 26

Busy with my small worries,
   I miss
      the Larger Answer.

. . . .

MAY 27

Pleasure weakens,
. . . Work strengthens.

. . . .

MAY 28

Violet,
    you hid so shyly
        beneath the green,
I didn't notice you!

. . . .

MAY 29

Daisy,
    I'll whisper a secret,
. . . if you promise not to tell!

. . . .

MAY 30

Empty of Knowledge,
. . . I have more room
. . . for Wonder!

. . . .

MAY 31

Three white lambs
    on a green lawn,
nibbling, nibbling,
    til it's all gone!

. . . .

JUNE

JUNE 1

The apple blossoms
      flutter to Earth,
. . . a white snow
      upon our green lawn.

. . . .

JUNE 2

Who is the queen of the garden?
Rose! I nominate *you!*

. . . .

JUNE 3

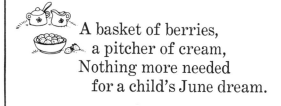

A basket of berries,
a pitcher of cream,
Nothing more needed
for a child's June dream.

· ·

JUNE 4

In the garden
of a lonely heart,
. . . a single perfect rose,
unseen.

· ·

JUNE 5

We cannot command
                 a Love,
We can only
               invite.

• •

JUNE 6

Let me keep Love
       in my heart,
ever ready for all
         tender things
           that grow
          ... and need.

• •

JUNE 7

Kindnesses
    are like seeds,
each begets another.

. . . .

JUNE 8

One rose,
  . . . and the Garden smiles!

. . . .

JUNE 9

Words
    can only hint
at what my heart feels,
    but cannot say.

. . . .

JUNE 10

What child's mind
    can keep to sums
When a robin's at the window
    and a June-time zephyr hums?

. . . .

JUNE 11

Without
      young boys,
Frogs
      would go
        greatly
          unappreciated!

• •

JUNE 12

Rain, you've spoiled our picnic!
Rain, you have ruined our day!
Rain, you were not invited...
Is *that* 'why' you've acted this way?

• •

JUNE 13

One leaf
    is Reason enough
        to Believe!

· ·

JUNE 14

Lily, . . . the regal bride of June.

· ·

JUNE 15

My heart is like a young fawn,
...shy in your presence.

· ·

JUNE 16

With my hand
        in yours,
I am no longer
        afraid.

· ·

JUNE 17

Reach out . . .
             touch!
Life is unpredictable,
   . . . and we are 'here,'
      Now!

. . . .

JUNE 18

We must each 'find' our Joys,
   as the child, in June,
      who hunts the sweet berries.

. . . .

JUNE 19

Little Kite,
    you walk across the clouds
      so easily,
. . . still holding *me*
    by the hand!

. . . .

JUNE 20

Within your glance
    sleeps a love
      I long to awaken.

. . . .

JUNE 21

Daisy! Daisy!
   ...golden face at my doorway!

. . . .

JUNE 22

A cup of seeds,
   a pinch of clover,
a berry dessert
   ...Robin's lunch is over!

. . . .

JUNE 23

A Sunset's
    mauve moment
        of Goodbye.

· ·

JUNE 24

Within the encircling silence,
    it is always
        my *own* voice
        I hear.

· ·

JUNE 25

Within a birthday basket,
    I peeked inside to see
one grey kitten, all alone,
    and it was just for *me!*

. . . .

JUNE 26

Child,
    what sunbeam
could warm me more
    than *your* smile?

. . . .

JUNE 27

Iris,
  where did you get
    such bright blue eyes?

. . . .

JUNE 28

As Stars populate the Night,
  As Daisies populate the fields,
  . . . so, thoughts of you
    populate my dreams.

. . . .

JUNE 29

To Each Day,
 ... its own Joy,
 ... its own Sorrow!

. . . .

JUNE 30

Bumble bee,
 ... Drowsy gentleman
  among my hollyhocks!

. . . .

JULY

JULY 1

Accept the gift
    of each new Day
        with a glad heart.

· ·

JULY 2

I watch
    the white voyage
        of a seagull
across
    a blank blue sky
and I know Peace.

· ·

JULY 3

In a vast auditorium of stars,
...a million clapping hands,
Oh, Sea!...what a wide
audience you are
for Midnight's dark drama.

. . . .

JULY 4

The answer is always
within ourselves.
Little soul...Search!

. . . .

JULY 5

When your love
        hurries to find me,
Oh! let me always
        be *there!*

. . . .

JULY 6

Hold my hand,
        and I can face
                tomorrow!

. . . .

JULY 7

Each sea shell
is
a tiny
curled-up
secret.

. . . .

JULY 8

The world is a family
of many members,
who squabble incessantly,
...as families *do!*

. . . .

JULY 9

Oh, my faithful friend,
. . . what happiness you
have brought me.

. . . .

JULY 10

The goldfish circle serenely
in their small crystal world,
. . . not a worry nor an enemy
in sight!

. . . .

JULY 11

The wild briar
     knows no Master.
He answers only
    . . . to the Wind,
      . . . and Sun.

. . . .

JULY 12

Men may die,
    but
        Mankind survives.

. . . .

JULY 13

We ask only "Harmony".
... and do not realize
      the measure of our request.

. . . .

JULY 14

The Sun, who's traveled all the Day,
    (He has so much to do!)
Now takes a cool dip in the Bay,
    (I'm sure that *I* would, too!)

. . . .

JULY 15

Tomorrow
is
ours!

. . . .

JULY 16

Yesterday bleats so loudly
in my ear,
. . . I cannot hear
Today!

. . . .

JULY 17

My thoughts
    are always near you.

. . . .

JULY 18

It is hot and dry
    upon this dusty summer road,
Yet, did I not also complain
    when it was muddy
with Spring rain?

. . . .

JULY 19

Lady-bug! Lady-bug
　　　. . . busy crimson mother
　　　　　in the tall green grass.

. . . .

JULY 20

Waves . . .
　　　Tiny thunders in a row,
like gnashing teeth
　　　crunching the sandy cookie
　　　　　of a shore.

. . . .

JULY 21

Wherever I walk,
          . . . though in a strange land,
the Earth and I are acquainted.

. . . .

JULY 22

It can never be again,
          . . . this moment!
Therefore, let me hold it
          carefully.

. . . .

JULY 23

Ecstasy
    is a butterfly.

. . . It will not stay!

. . . .

JULY 24

A true friend
    loves us for our faults
        as well as for our virtues!

. . . .

JULY 25

How gently
    the rain
cools
      the hot brow
        of a Summer hill.

. . . .

JULY 26

Hope comes shyly
    through the gate,
Stands at my door
    . . . and beckons!

. . . .

JULY 27

The sea is a meadow of green,
   where white daisies bloom, now,
      atop the billows.

. . . .

JULY 28

And if love comes . . .
   catch it!

It may not come again!

. . . .

JULY 29

Oh!
   ...what happened
      to Yesterday?

. . . .

JULY 30

How dark my day
   When you leave it,
...like a garden
      When the sun departs.

. . . .

JULY 31

Who is ever too "old"
for ice cream?

. . . .

AUGUST

AUGUST 1

I am always
   in a hurry...
Oh, World, *wait!*

. . . .

AUGUST 2

Kindness dissolves an anger
   as Water dissolves the rock.

. . . .

AUGUST 3

Though he may devise
    a multitude of distractions,
no man can long avoid *himself!*

. . . .

AUGUST 4

Beside the careless roadside,
Each daisy has a dusty hem.

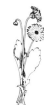

. . . .

AUGUST 5

The carnation stands astonished,
  in pink ruffles ...
like a startled ballerina,
  upon a summer stage.

. . . .

AUGUST 6

The life of a firefly
  is of little consequence,
but how silverly it decorates
  this dark scarf of night.

. . . .

AUGUST 7

We must Believe,
   . . . or nothing Begins.

. . . .

AUGUST 8

Little fish,
   . . . be warned,
Big fish
   are always hungry!

. . . .

AUGUST 9

Doctor,
      what is the cure
        for Love?

. . . .

AUGUST 10

In the darkness,
   . . . a Light!
   . . . *your* love,
      twinkling
         through despair!

. . . .

AUGUST 11

Little bird, with broken wing,
you cannot fly,
... but you *can* "sing".

. . . .

AUGUST 12

Sweet wishes wing
along their way,
from me to you,
... to start your day.

. . . .

AUGUST 13

Though you are far away,
 Memory holds you near.

. . . .

AUGUST 14

Lazily, my paper fan
 stirs the air
 on this breathless afternoon.

. . . .

AUGUST 15

Like a hidden spring,
    your love has nourished me,
        through all the arid hours.

. . . .

AUGUST 16

Three black crows
    Upon a blue sky
And one white cloud
    . . . sauntering by.

. . . .

AUGUST 17

What child
    does not rejoice at lollipops?
Which one
    resists a jelly-bean?

. . . .

AUGUST 18

Life has its seasons
    as surely as the Earth's,
Yet how we struggle to detain them!

. . . .

AUGUST 19

Sunset!
  Goodbye to the face
    that makes each Day bright,
And hello to the stars,
    and dear Father night.

. . . .

AUGUST 20

Bright Zinnia
    brings us thoughts
        of absent friends.

. . . .

AUGUST 21

Nothing
    can stop us...
If we're *together!*

. . . .

AUGUST 22

Rosemary,
    ... for sweet remembrance.

. . . .

AUGUST 23

This morning is 'new',
  . . . but I have 'old' thoughts
      in my head!

. . . .

AUGUST 24

Caught in a jar,
      too delicate to hold,
The firefly flashes
      his signal of 'gold.'

. . . .

AUGUST 25

 Watermelon,
...Summer's sweetest gift!

. . . .

AUGUST 26

Life sings to us,
    whether we listen or not.

. . . .

AUGUST 27

I love you
even when
I may not
like
you!

. . . .

AUGUST 28

Pick a cherry,
—pick a few,
Summer's made them
just for you!

. . . .

AUGUST 29

Nothing quite so succulent
as a tart ripe plum,
Frosty from a cool crock,
won't you bring me one?

. . . .

AUGUST 30

We leave our island summer,
reluctantly,
our sun-brown bodies
uncomfortable, now,
in city clothes.

. . . .

AUGUST 31

A poem
is a moment 'remembered',
...in words!

· ·

SEPTEMBER

SEPTEMBER 1

How wealthy
   are the Autumn hills
      with September's gold!

· · · · · · · · · · · · · · · · · · · ·

SEPTEMBER 2

Books
  are
    silent friends.

· · · · · · · · · · · · · · · · · · · ·

SEPTEMBER 3

He who finds no delight in flowers
must be a chilly soul, indeed!

. . . .

SEPTEMBER 4

Each night we die,
. . . to be born, anew
with every rising sun.

. . . .

SEPTEMBER 5

After long holidays
    it is always pleasant
       to arrive again
          at one's *own* front door!

. . . .

SEPTEMBER 6

As the Sunflower
       follows the Sun,
So, faithfully,
      my thoughts tend
          ever towards you.

. . . .

SEPTEMBER 7

Back to school! Back to school,
   go the girls and boys
As they leave behind them
   Summer, fun, and toys.

. . . .

SEPTEMBER 8

Little dream,
   we have been together
   for so *long* a time,

I cannot exchange you, *now*,
   for a Reality!

. . . .

SEPTEMBER 9

How sticky the mind
    that is Discontent.

. . . .

SEPTEMBER 10

Your voice,
    . . . my only music,
your smile,
    . . . my only sun.

. . . .

SEPTEMBER 11

 Even the weed
      at the roadside
has its moment
      of flowering.

. . . .

SEPTEMBER 12

How Sad,
   . . . to leave a Summer!
How Chill,
   . . . to start a Fall!

. . . .

SEPTEMBER 13

Whose beads are these
        upon the tree . . . ?
Rain spills her jewels
        so carelessly!

. . . .

SEPTEMBER 14

When you're basically
    a messy person,
Neatness can be a strain.

. . . .

SEPTEMBER 15

 Groups of grapes,
purple-sweet,
September's annual
amethyst treat.

. . . .

SEPTEMBER 16

Few men
mention their benefits,
But most men
mention their woes!

. . . .

SEPTEMBER 17

Peering, ever,
        into the eyes of strangers,
    . . . is it not
            myself I seek?

. . . .

SEPTEMBER 18

A false friend
        is like the morning dew,
    . . . how quickly they leave
        when things get
            'warmer'!

. . . .

SEPTEMBER 19

No Tears, Dear Friends,
. . . Enjoy!

· ·

SEPTEMBER 20

I always intend to forget you,
. . . but I never do!

· ·

SEPTEMBER 21

It is difficult
    to be sad,
When a morning sun
    shines in your window.

. . . .

SEPTEMBER 22

Oh! the mystery of numbers!
    Oh!... the labyrinth of sums!

. . . .

SEPTEMBER 23

Haystack, haystack,
...golden hill,
We all climb Up,
    then Down we spill!

. . . .

SEPTEMBER 24

Work willingly
    or not at all,
...Reluctance makes
    a slow teammate.

. . . .

SEPTEMBER 25

Love sweetens
any disposition!

. . . .

SEPTEMBER 26

The orchard boughs
are bent low
with September
fruitfulness.

. . . .

SEPTEMBER 27

Day dreaming
is my best
subject!

· ·

SEPTEMBER 28

Live each day fully,
as though there would be
no others.

· ·

SEPTEMBER 29

September starts so greenly
    and ends so goldenly.

. . . .

SEPTEMBER 30

Down they come,
    . . . my summer friends.

. . . .

OCTOBER

OCTOBER 1

The sunshine
of a smile
can melt
the frostiest countenance.

. . . .

OCTOBER 2

October
is
a carnival of Color!

. . . .

OCTOBER 3

Chrysanthemums, like shaggy lions,
roam the edges of our garden.

. . . .

OCTOBER 4

People expect too much
of each other!

. . . .

OCTOBER 5

Sometimes
    I feel so alone!

. . . .

OCTOBER 6

It's time to rake the leaves away,
It's time to pile them high,
Upon their fragrant mounds we play,
. . .'til sunset's in the sky.

. . . .

OCTOBER 7

Bring the baskets,
  Bring the cart,
It's Harvest-Time...
  Come! Let us start!

. . . .

OCTOBER 8

With leafy whispers
  the forest speaks,
...oh! that *I* could spill
  such soft words!

. . . .

OCTOBER 9

Never withold a tenderness.
Oh! *Speak* the love you feel!

. . . .

OCTOBER 10

The pumpkin
   is October's smile...
Such golden grins,
   ...for mile on mile.

. . . .

OCTOBER 11

 Dandelion
    in the Fall,
Is a white balloon
    with string and all!

. . . .

OCTOBER 12

Oh, my love,
Sunrise and Sunset,
    your song
        is always
           with me!

. . . .

OCTOBER 13

One day,
I should like to be
self-confident!

. . . .

OCTOBER 14

We have a tiny mouse
Who's living in our house.
Unless *he* goes away,
I'm sure that *I* won't stay!

. . . .

OCTOBER 15

 How sad
        is the drooping aster,
once she's kissed
        by Frost.

. . . .

OCTOBER 16

Oh, the hills speak,
        and I must Listen.
The wind calls,
        . . . and I must hear!

. . . .

OCTOBER 17

Each of us
  needs the reassurance
    that a kind word can bring.

. . . .

OCTOBER 18

Anger pecks at Happiness,
  as the black crow pecks
    the sweet pear
  ...leaving its beauty
    pierced, and marred!

. . . .

OCTOBER 19

Jack O'Lantern,
. . . orange friend!
smiling, . . . glowing,
. . . til the end!

. . . .

OCTOBER 20

Everyone else
seems to know
all the Answers.
While *I* am
still asking
the Questions!

. . . .

OCTOBER 21

Be happy
in this day you have
been given...
We have so little time!
Do not waste it,
complaining!

. . . .

OCTOBER 22

I try not
to decide anything
that can wait
til later.

. . . .

OCTOBER 23

 Whose
little Pumpkin
are *You?*

. . . .

OCTOBER 24

Oh, my friend!
How happy were the days
When we were *together!*

. . . .

OCTOBER 25

Ideas, like seeds, are many...
   but each must find root
      in the long unhurrying soil
      ...of Time!

. . . .

OCTOBER 26

The barren trees
    stand impoverished, now,
       by October,
Who were so rich
    ...in June.

. . . .

OCTOBER 27

Farewell, Farewell,
  We shall not see Robin again
  Til another March shall come!

. . . .

OCTOBER 28

The birds are flying overhead,
  The oak leaves turn
    to brown and red,
The air is frosty... Pumpkin's here,
  The days grow short
    ...November's near!

. . . .

OCTOBER 29

Though
     you forget,
Still,
    I remember!

. . . .

OCTOBER 30

Sentinel squirrel,
   high in the oak,
. . . what a fluffy flag
   you wave!

. . . .

OCTOBER 31

Beneath the sheet
    march two little feet.
Behind the mask
    "Who's there?" I ask.

NOVEMBER

NOVEMBER 1

And now,
. . . A rush of wild geese
      triangled toward the South.

. . . .

NOVEMBER 2

Yesterday flies
    with the withered leaves,
. . . never to be retrieved!

. . . .

NOVEMBER 3

November
...how grey
is your attire!

. . . .

NOVEMBER 4

Where are the rubies
the apple trees owned?
Oh! gone is the gold
of the oak!

. . . .

NOVEMBER 5

Worries hurry through my mind
    like dark flocks of birds
        through an Autumn sky.

. . . .

NOVEMBER 6

Oh, my friends,
    be not down-hearted,
Surely tomorrow
    must be better!

. . . .

NOVEMBER 7

Which Day begins
   without some 'promise'?

. . . .

NOVEMBER 8

We always admire
the wisdom of
   those who agree
      with us.

. . . .

NOVEMBER 9

 A Diary
        is a Treasure-House
         of Secrets.

. . . .

NOVEMBER 10

In November,
   the Sun
      is a timid
         visitor.

. . . .

NOVEMBER 11

Far from other Voices
I find my stillness
    . . . and my Answer.

. . . .

NOVEMBER 12

Our sleek black cat
    poses in a sunset window,
Knowing the graceful
    portrait she creates.

. . . .

NOVEMBER 13

Remnants of Time,
       that is all I have,
But I shall stitch them to Beauty
   with a patchwork persistence.

. . . .

NOVEMBER 14

Knowing little,
   I am an appreciative
              listener!

. . . .

NOVEMBER 15

Wishing
is
my
Happiest
Occupation!

. . . .

NOVEMBER 16

Oh, my distant friend,
take up your pen,
. . . and 'talk' to me!

. . . .

NOVEMBER 17

How stalwart is the tiny tug-boat
pulling his string of heavy barges
down the Bay!
Let us be as steadfast!

. . . .

NOVEMBER 18

Such a little word,
. . . yet so hard to say,
. . . No!

. . . .

NOVEMBER 19

I *meant*
   to be wise . . .
but, perhaps,
   that was 'foolish' of me!

. . . .

NOVEMBER 20

A Friend brings sunlight
   to the darkest day.

. . . .

NOVEMBER 21

 Thanksgiving
     is a moment of prayers,
       . . . and wishbones!

. . . .

NOVEMBER 22

Oh, Memory,
    Stay not awake
      on such a dreary Midnight!

. . . .

NOVEMBER 23

So timid is my dream
  ...Perhaps your kindness
   may shelter it.

· ·

NOVEMBER 24

No matter
  how I hurry,
 ...I am always behind!

· ·

NOVEMBER 25

Life,
   I love you . . .
but you 'hurry' so!

. . . .

NOVEMBER 26

Don't be afraid to trust.
   Love, like a strong wave,
      will carry, and support you!

. . . .

NOVEMBER 27

In my head
        the armies battle!
. . . but I seldom know who 'wins'!

. . . .

NOVEMBER 28

On the darkest days
. . . who comes to cheer me?
                . . . Chickadee!

. . . .

NOVEMBER 29

Catch the moments
as they fly,
. . . they do not come *again!*

. . . .

NOVEMBER 30

You awaken Long Dreams
in me,
that Duty does not
allow me
to finish.

. . . .

DECEMBER

DECEMBER 1

In December,
are we not *all*
"children," wishing?

· ·

DECEMBER 2

Sometimes,
it is Wisdom
to be Foolish!

· ·

DECEMBER 3

Out of a cold world
    I walked into a warm room,

... It was your love!

. . . .

DECEMBER 4

As green as the holly
    that does not change,
my love for you
        shall ever be.

. . . .

DECEMBER 5

I stand in awe
at the majesty
of a single star!

. . . .

DECEMBER 6

Pink nose
and prickly toes,
that's the way
December goes!

. . . .

DECEMBER 7

How wise, though cold,
    ... the undreaming heart!

. . . .

DECEMBER 8

Oh, Winter!
... I *knew* you would come,
    but not so *soon!*

. . . .

DECEMBER 9

At last...
    the white benediction
        of snow.

. . . .

DECEMBER 10

Always alert to the clamour
    of Danger and Discord,
We are sometimes unmindful
    of the softer sounds,
       . . . of Beauty,
          and of Love.

. . . .

DECEMBER 11

Now,
    Winter's icy claws
        have caught
            the hurrying brook,
and all is still.

. . . .

DECEMBER 12

Snowman
. . . Winter's
    sudden
      friend.

. . . .

DECEMBER 13

A winter kitchen
    filled with the aroma
        of freshly-baked bread...
        there is no *better* perfume!

. . . .

DECEMBER 14

My heart
    still sings
The song
    you taught it.

. . . .

DECEMBER 15

The snow is a thin white thread
    slowly stitching the grey afghan
       of a meadow.

. . . .

DECEMBER 16

Often, it is the wandering path
    that leads
        most quickly
         Home!

. . . .

DECEMBER 17

The mistletoe is hung...
come, my love,
    let me taste your kiss.

. . . .

DECEMBER 18

We are not apart.
...Though Separate,
    yet, we are near.
Love easily knits
    the Two to One.

. . . .

DECEMBER 19

Only *I*
     can begin
          the Peace
     that
          must
               be.

. . . .

DECEMBER 20

Now, in the winter wind,
   our solemn pines suddenly sing
in an emerald chorus.

. . . .

DECEMBER 21

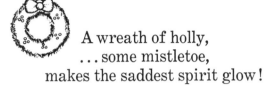

A wreath of holly,
... some mistletoe,
makes the saddest spirit glow!

. . . .

DECEMBER 22

Hear the bells!
  Oh, hear them chime!
Ring out the news ...
  It's Christmastime!

. . . .

DECEMBER 23

All things
    seem Impossible,
... until
    they are Done!

· · · · · · · · · · · · · · · · · · · ·

DECEMBER 24

See the star
    Let all Believe,
Tell near and Far
    ... It's Christmas Eve!

· · · · · · · · · · · · · · · · · · · ·

DECEMBER 25

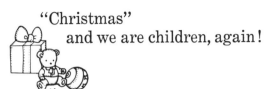

"Christmas"
and we are children, again!

. . . .

DECEMBER 26

Time hurries past,
. . . but memories remain.

. . . .

DECEMBER 27

And now,
    Another Dawn
        blushes
            behind the pine!

. . . .

DECEMBER 28

Each man is his own best helper.

. . . .

DECEMBER 29

Sometimes,
Morning
comes
too early!

. . . .

DECEMBER 30

Time
promises
Nothing.
. . . except
this
moment!

. . . .

DECEMBER 31

I hate endings!

NOTES

NOTES